YOUR KNOWLEDGE HAS VALUE

AF139807

- We will publish your bachelor's and
  master's thesis, essays and papers

- Your own eBook and book -
  sold worldwide in all relevant shops

- Earn money with each sale

Upload your text at www.GRIN.com
and publish for free

Bibliographic information published by the German National Library:

The German National Library lists this publication in the National Bibliography; detailed bibliographic data are available on the Internet at http://dnb.dnb.de .

Imprint:

Copyright © 2017 GRIN Verlag
Print and binding: Books on Demand GmbH, Norderstedt Germany
ISBN: 9783668754119

This book at GRIN:

https://www.grin.com/document/418401

Henry Louis Sterling Appleyard

Sexual Alias. Mediatisation of Desire in Social Network Services

GRIN Verlag

Table of Contents

Sexual Alias
Mediatisation of Desire in Social Network Services

Introduction

The relationship between sexuality and communication technologies is changing. In media life, people are increasingly seeing themselves and others through the social network service (SNS). Social media users "sign up" their name, age, and sex before they have access. Once attained, the user is afforded a 'configurable networked self' (Cohen, 2015:69) that is voluntarily serviced with and *within* the social network. With growing aspects of use, especially in younger people to 'communicate their own life story' (Larsen, 2016:24), the SNS poses and imposes differential user-experiences rooted in media logics.

For media to embed its logic into social-sexual practice it must contend with deep human emotions or 'sub-processes' that are at the core of psychological development; 'how people understand themselves, how do they think of themselves; do they label themselves, and do they announce or enact that identity to an audience or in a social setting?' (Plante, 2006:200). A person's sexuality then, their gender expression and identity, are part of one's developed (sub)consciousness. Principled archetypes - the socio-cultural norms and values of femininity and masculinity - are violently in flux. Under the integration of social media into social life the psychological recognition and reconfiguration of one's sex i.e, their sexual identity(s), orientation, fantasies, feelings, behaviors, and desires (weeks 2011), are becoming part of an assemblage of interdependent media networks.

As Walgrave et al (2016) lament, such logistics change 'how the characteristics of SNSs accommodate needs inherent to adolescent development [which] may explain why adolescents have rapidly and enthusiastically integrated SNSs into their daily lives' (p.124). The evolving characteristics of SNSs are not only dependent on active interactional and communicative needs executed *within* the service but also produce differential user experiences based on the information supplied with the service.

The paper investigates this phenomenon, specifically how age, location and/or sex effects the *Facebook* SNS user experience – to explore the relatively uncharted territory of *how new media logics symbiotically service people's desires as a form of media-embedded practices*. Given the complexity of the research topic, the paper breaks into five parts - Mediatisation of Sexuality; Facebook User Analysis; Deconstructing the Alias; Social Network Sexualities; Mediatisation Desire – grappling with notions of a mediatised sexual alias.

Mediatisation and Sexuality

People now sexually communicate through media-embedded socio-sexual practices afforded and accommodated with the use of SNSs. Like with other aspects of mediatisation research (Ekstrom et al. 2016; Deuze 2014; Mazzoleni & Shultz 1999), media-embedded processes driving sociocultural change are becoming the norm. The rise and integration of computer-mediated communication (CMC) have proliferated a data mine of social and cultural capital that the SNS has used to appropriate itself into public/private spheres.

Now 'perceived as cultural properties as well as social technics' (Jansson, 2015:2), the SNS inhibits mediatisational processes, changing the psychological development of sexual self-determination and self-identification. Related work points to de Ridder's (2015; 2017) mediatisation approach to sexuality, asking 'why media matter to people's sexualities and how people value their sexual lives in, with or around media' (p.19). Warning of a 'radical ontological change in how we look at processes of communication, mainly mass communication and culture,' de Ridder calls attention to 'Facebook (now used by an ever-increasing number of people around the world to communicate sexual identity).

Sexuality and sexual identity(s) are now an embedded media practice. Hilton-Morrow & Battles, (2015) introduces sexuality as a categorization process. Sexual identity and language are constructed and managed, 'continually in flux as cultural meanings are continually negotiated' (p. 10). This negotiating of norms in the construction and management of sexual identity on SNS presents an insightful perspective into media-embedded forces that normalize certain behaviors, orientations, and desires.

The Service

The social media service (SNS) is a symbiotic relationship between user wants and service needs i.e., social media institutions 'provide stability and meaning to social behavior' (Scott, 2012:15) whilst relying on the expropriation of such behaviors to service user wants, motivations and desires. This is to encourage meaningful user-generation and mediation, giving the service more social and cultural capital. Given the nature of the social media site and the induced processes of meditation as outlined, the social network service would be a better approximation. The use of an identity service, or 'identity workshop' (Wakeford 2003), implies the voluntary, participatory and cooperative motion that a user undertakes.

The SNS, like the servicing of an automobile, brings with it notions of a certain set of skills or tools that are hired and utilized. Unlike the automobile service, however, the form of capital is socio-cultural – if one transacts their personhood online they are free to use the service. The user needs to go through a process of mediatisation in order to embed their social practices and identity in the service e.g. like an automobile needs a WOF. When a user registers to a service, their information is crosschecked as part of a wider network that authenticates and verifies the transaction. As we will explore, the SNS also crosschecks a user's information when they sign up their name, age, and sex. After passing, the user is then prompted to generate or "repair" their newborn social media life: uploading more content, being suggested posts, tweets, photos, friends, groups and so on. These suggestions or "recommendations" by the service advises and guides a user to their experiential evaluations, granting them tools and utilities dependent on their incentive saliency.

Granted with "toolhood" (Heller and Goodman, 2016), the user utilises the SNS as a manageable substitute for offline interpersonal interaction and identification. This symbiotic relationship is programming an online performing persona that uses social networking mechanisms to

Figure removed due to copyright issues

Figure 1

comfortably and neatly control their social life. This is seeing a growing phantasmatic attachment to SNSs, currently dominated by *Facebook* (Fig.1), providing a finely-tuned tool for identification, presentation and impression management. The service's 'identity workshop' is extensive and constantly being updated and reconfigured - a saliently desirable 'pipeline of experience' (Mark Zuckerberg in 2014) – narrated by the user but plotted by the platform.

Within the SNS users narrate or "self-qualifies" their own life story, held in juxtaposition to the computational and media logics that quantify these life stories in code. The socio-cultural frequency or quality of the information shared with the SNS service, like sexuality, are connected to complex interpersonal psychological developments that are being oversimplified or aliased, under algorithmic processes. As Iliadis & Federica Russo lament (2015), organisations like SNSs 'own vast quantities of user information and hold lucrative data capital, wield algorithms and data processing tools with the ability to influence emotions and culture.' (p.1).

Aliasing and Algorithms

Unlike the user's social media presence, profile or persona, the user's *alias* is this distortion or under-sampled version of configurable Self. Traditionally used to define how distortion occurs when processing images, film, and sound, 'aliasing arises when a signal is discretely sampled at a rate that is insufficient to capture the changes in the signal' (Olshausen, 2000 p.1). Through aliasing, the self-qualifying 'signal takes on a different persona or a false presentation due to being sampled at an insufficiently high frequency' (p.2). This 'algorithmic identity' (Cheney-Lippold, 2011) is an evolutionary part of a weapon of *math* destruction, where 'all knowledge - past, present, and future - can be derived from data by a single, universal algorithm' (Domingos, 2015:27).

Machine-learning algorithms now station the communicative highways of the Internet (Google 2017). Data is centralising around cloud technologies and services that implement such algorithms; 'using both simple and complex sorting mechanisms at the same time, they combine high-level description, an embedded command structure, and mathematical formulae that can be written in various programming languages' (Roberge & Seyfert 2016). These programming languages are only fluent to a small few who have studied the computational programming of algorithmic cultures – talents of which have been soaked by big data empires. These largely misunderstood mechanisms are driving ubiquitous media futures in which those with the highest capacity of algorithmic logics and control embody an overarching command structure.

These media structures are the new multi-dimensional gatekeepers, calculating, processing and reasoning internetworked alias produce an autonomous and effectual method of computation. The entrenched alias is thus part of the deterministic mesh of non-human forces that is prefigured through the pedagogical consumption for the machine- learning algorithms. – 'creating an algorithm unfolds in context through processes such as trail and error, play, collaboration and negotiation' (Roberge & Seyfert, 2016:10).

Facebook's Alias

Before we proceed with the user Analyses of SNS Facebook, we must take a critical look at where the company is situated when it comes to potential ties with other networks. The Facebook alias, as part of a neoliberal postcapitalist 'algorithmic ideology' (Mayer 2012), is owned, privatised, and profiteered off

Driving and aggregating more web traffic than Google (Ingram 2015), *Facebook* (previously *Facemash*) will have more than 2 billion users interacting and communicating with the service by 2018 (Petro 2012). The *Facebook* alias is part of a vast interworked conglomerate valued at $100 billion; currently owned by

Facemash creator Mark Zuckerberg, *Accel Partner* investment founder Jim Breyer, mobile sharing site *Path* ' s Dustin Moskovitz, Uri Milner of *Digital Sky* investments, *Napster*'s Sean Parker, *Paypal* founder Peter Theil and even *Microsoft's* Bill Gates (Dunlop 2017). Along with connections to data mining and profiling companies *Datalogix, Epsilon, Acxiom,* and *BlueKai,* the *Facebook* alias also joins the network of over 50 companies including social media services *Messenger, Instagram, WhatsApp, ConnectU, LuckyCal* and interactive firms *Wildfire Interactive* and *Oculus Rift.*

As Goodwin (2016) lament, 'an average of over 1,000 minutes per month are now spent on it by its users. For many, most notably users in eastern Asia, *Facebook* is not just the Internet – it's bigger than the Internet. With servers farms that scale to 487,000-square foot (Data Center Knowledge 2016), *Facebook* is restructuring the data trails and traffic of the Internet. The SNS processes at least '2.5 billion pieces of content and 500+ terabytes of data each day...pulling in 2.7 billion "Like" actions and 300 million photos per day, and it scans roughly 105 terabytes of data each half hour' (Constine 2012). The *Facebook* alias evolves through such "like", or desirable, actions taken in one's social media life, with the user's data - name, age, location, and sex - being utilised for "experiential reprogramming". *Facebook's* new underwater cable Marea put down this year has a capacity to transfer such data at 160 terabits *per second* - "this one cable will be able to do almost half of what all the cables do" (Markman 2016).

The Facebook alias is thus the key to unlocking how and why SNS like Facebook use the socio-cultural capital they acquire, adapting and accommodating the interpolation of their user's desires. Facebook uses aliased information to target different social groups, loaning out social capital to, say, 'disadvantaged youth seek[ing] to connect and expand their networks well beyond their limited social capital' (Arora & Scheiber, 2017).

Researchers have found that heteronormative forces (Boryczka, 2017; Phipps et al. 2017) have migrated online (Antin & Cheshire, 2011) although little research is focused on how socio-cultural understandings of sexuality have translated (and aliased). After starting with a predominantly male user base,

Figure removed due to copyright issues

Figure 2

in the 2008 *Facebook* saw female users suddenly and protectively become the majority (Fig. 2). During this time *Facebook* was opened to the free market and self-proclaimed feminist Sheryl Sandberg was hired as the COO, posing questions to how market forces and such a socio-sexual perspective influenced the direction of the service. At the time Facebook's profits were stumbling, now the company is generating hundreds of billions in profits through market analyses and advertisement. One direction Facebook took, was to do a complete overhaul of their affordances and features, one of which was "options for discovery" in the form suggested pages, people, and groups. The suggestions produced are steeped in mathematical code and required analyses from the "inside-out".

Facebook User Analyses

With its consistent hold on the network as outlined and driving more web traffic than *Google* (Ingram 2015), *Facebook* will be the analytical site in which the SNS will be investigated. Under controlled conditions, this study artificially manufactured *Facebook* aliases online to see how the service's "options for discovery" differentiates depending on age, location and/or sex.

Using an analysis of the "top suggested" groups and related tags that *Facebook's* algorithm formulates will shed some light on the 'algorithmic ideology' (Mayer, 2012) employed. With each being the opposite sex, ages chosen included 13 (requirement age) and 25 (average age of user). These two age categories are focal points for *Facebook*, striving to sign up new users as well as maintaining their most numerous. It must be noted that *Facebook* requires either the binary choice of male or female before the user can configure their social media Self and experience.

This test is to trial how *Facebook's* affordances and suggestions differ from purely age, sex and/or location of a user. There was no uploading or interacting with the network. The only information that was supplied only included what was required to sign up: email/phone number, name, age, birthday and the choice between female and male.

Conventional emails were created (*Outlook, Yahoo, Google, AOL*) as well as convincing names (Jenny Taylor, Robert Smith, Margret Jones, John Williamson), which could or could not have an effect. All users access Facebook on the same day (2/5/2017), with the same web browser (*Google Chrome*) over the course of 6 hours with screenshots being used to document each user experience. Along with Jodi Dean (2003), the paper hypotheses that 'we might expect a social media tailored to individualism, competition, alliance, entertainment, and pro-creation' (p.2).

Controlled Conditions

Site of Access

Facebook's algorithm can behave differently depending on the GPS location of where a user is logging in from i.e., for now, home computer, tablet or mobile. The number of different students that would use University library computers, as well as the server-based login system, provide a level of anonymity that would be impossible from a personal computer.

Signing up each user's *Facebook* alias was done from a different University library computer (IP address) under the "guest-login" account. All cookies (website files that store user-specific information) and caches (file 'images' web browser stores) will be deleted prior. This is to help mask the user's identity whilst interacting with the service, which could or could not have an effect.

VPN (Virtual Private Network)

By use of programs such as *Hola (Google Chrome* extension), VPN can change the IP address of a computer to act if it is a different country. This makes *Facebook* act as if that user is accessing the platform from the chosen country, in this case, America (US) and New Zealand (NZ).

Under such rapid growth as outlined, VPN was used to see if demographical "hot-spots" change the user experience of a given country. Differences in *Facebook's* suggestions dependent on nationalities offer a socio-cultural lens through which the service operates and accommodates.

Group Categories and Table Comparison

Six group categories were chosen with respect to the related tags that Facebook associates with that particular category e.g. Relationship with Love. This approach led to a couple of categories for NZ (Women and Gender) to be different from US (Marriage and Dating).

With sex at the top and group categories down the left column, the table displays Facebook's top 4 suggested groups followed by the 10 related tags in *numerical order*. The category groups and related tags that correspond across both sexes (*Table 1* and 2) and countries (*Table 3*) have been highlighted. Although most results speak for themselves, we will then do a brief evaluation of each comparison.

TABLE 1
AGE:13
LOCATION:NZ

	FEMALE	MALE
IDENTITY AND RELATIONSHIPS	1. New Zealand Adult Singles 2. Positive Men and Women friendship group 3. Ladies Advice (new mums, old mums) 4. Cheaper living (NZ only!) Friendships; Single parent; Weddings; Love; Family; Marriage; Women; **Relationships**; LGTB; Wedding Photography	1. Medical Musings with Friends 2. The Mum Hub 3. Buy & Sell PRELOVED Wedding Goods 4. Cheaper Living (NZ only!) Friendships; Love; Weddings; Family; Marriage; Dating; Women; Socialising; LGTB; Wedding Photography
RELATIONSHIPS	1. Everything Lady Like 2. Soul Sisters 3. Magnetic Women club 4. Facebook Friends Love; Dating; Marriage; Friendship; Women; Online-dating service; Polyamory; Spirituality; Singles group; Romance	1. Secret Men's Business 2. Legit 18+ Singles Lookn for Friendship 3. Awakened Singles NZ 4. DarkSide Singles 18+ (")
LOVE	1. Real Men Treat Their Women like princesses 2. Not ashamed of Jesus Christ 3. Beautiful People Connect 4. In Love With Nature Friendship; Dating; Relationships; Marriage; Relationship; Happiness; God; Music: Spirituality	1. The Australian Way of the Superior Man 2. Singles & Solos Haven NZ 3. LGBT 4. Beautiful People Connect (")
FRIENDSHIP	1. Beautiful People Connect 2. Facebook Real friends 3. Anjos 4. HEART OF FACEBOOK Love: Dating; Family: Chatear; Music; Funny; Support; Having fun; Happiness; Relationships	1. I Am Looking For YOU… 2. Empowering uniqueness 3. Singles & Solos Haven NZ 4. Beautiful People Connect (")
WOMEN	1. New Girlfriends 2. Women's International Creative-group 3. World Travelistas 4. Gutsy Women Circle Entrepreneurship; Empowerment; Networking; Business; Christian; Friendship; Leader; Feminism; Spirituality; Love	1. Equal Opportunity Science - Australia (")
GENDER	1. Early Ultrasound Gender Prediction…(?) 2. Strictly Nub Theory 3. Ultra Violet 4. Gender Dysphoria/Transgender Support Feminism; Transgender; Sexuality; Politics; LGBT; Human rights; Education; LGBT culture	1. Trans IQ2ed (")

TABLE 2
AGE:13
LOCATION:
USA

	FEMALE	MALE
IDENTITY AND RELATIONSHIPS	1. Foreigners looking for Filipina 2. US visa applications 3. Asian Dating Looking for a Serious Relationship 4. USA and Europe love Pinay ladies Friendships; Love; Dating; Marriage; Family; Girlfriend; Divorce; Online Dating Service; Single Parent	1. Sweet Indian Girls 2. Human Friends International 3. BBW, Plus Size Singles, Big Women/Men 4. Naughty Dating Love; Friendships; Marriage; Dating; Family; Women; Scorpio; Romance; Women; Engagement; Capricorn
RELATIONSHIPS	1. The Divorce Support Group 2. Reflections on Relationships 3. Singles ladies that want a committed man 4. Born Again Love; Dating; Marriage; Friendship; Women; Online-dating service; Polyamory; Spirituality; Singles group; Romance	1. Secret Men's Business 2. Born Again 3. Esoteric Tantra 4. Flame Couples Ministry (")
LOVE	1. Singles- Dating – Friendship Worldwide 2. Single Christian men and women for mature relationships 3. Filipina women meet foreign men 4. Take My Breath Away Friendship; Dating; Relationships; Marriage; Relationship; Happiness; God; Music: Spirituality; Family	1. Hot Zone+ 18 2. Secrets 3. Exotic Dating 4. Love and dating with girls (")
FRIENDSHIP	1. Dairy of an RP 2.0 2. Filipina women meet foreign men 3. Dairy of an RP 4. International Friendship Love: Dating; Family: Chatear; Music; Funny; Support; Having fun; Happiness; Relationships	1. Find new music. Fans for artists 2. Exotic Dating 3. Add Friendly People & Posts 4. Friendship Point (")
MARRIAGE	1. Other Women, Wives and Ladies 2. Filipina Looking For Serious Relationships 3. Love and Dating in Hong Kong 4. Single Christian men and women for mature relationships Love; Relationships; Dating; Weddings; Relationship; Friendship; Parenting; Christianity; Wife; Family	1. Le café 2. International Dating for Relationships 3. Femdom Marriage 4. Revert Muslims Want Marry (")
DATING	1. Love me with all of your Heart 2. Asian Beauties for Serious Friendships 3. Meet Christian Singles Dating or Friendship Site 4. Single Ready to mix and mingle Love; Friendship; Chatear; Relationships; Friendship; Marriage; Online Dating Service; Singles group; Singles; Single Women	1. Personal Development, Dating & Lifestyle 2. Best Adult Dating Websites 3. Naughty Dating 4. Euro Flirt (")

Age:13

Findings

Upon being "born" on *Facebook*, both female and male 13-year-olds

are greeted synonymously. First, a verification code is sent to either

an email or telephone. Facebook then asks for another email as the

service had back checked the email provided and found no connections. After clicking skip, Facebook has

an automated response for someone who doesn't have any connections (above). The service then asks for

a profile picture to be uploaded, as well as the full customisation of the home page, bio, and settings in

general. The only graphic user interface (GUI) affordances that differed between the two sexes was,

curiously, that on the homepage after clicking 'discover groups' there appeared to be a 'create group' button

only for the male (Fig. 1) and not the female (Fig. 2). Accessing the same account from the US, however,

showed that the 'create group' available to female. This poses questions of whether there is any bias whilst

updated certain firmware, features etc.

Figure removed due to copyright issues   *Figure removed due to copyright issues*

Figure 1   *Figure 2*

New Zealand (NZ)

The analysis found that the female group suggestions were more sexualised, with groups such as 'New

Zealand Adult Singles' (236 members) being compared to the male's 'Medical Musings with Friends' (962.

We can see clearly that Facebook does not aggregate the groups with the highest membership – second to

'New Zealand Adult Singles' is 'Positive Men and Women friendship' (5,208) - actively suggesting groups

that are not by popular demand. Principled female and male stereotypes are clearly visible with 'Secret

Men's Business' (in juxtaposition to 'Everything Lady Like'. This becomes more obvious with the first

suggested group under 'Love' being 'Real Men Treat Their Women like princesses' as oppose to 'The

Australian Way of the Superior Man'. For an Australian group to come up with a New Zealand user analysis suggests that Facebook's algorithm centralises around larger and more active demographics. Strong emotive language displayed with titles like 'Facebook Real Friends' or the 'HEART OF FACEBOOK'. More on the male side, individualistic norms and conventions displayed with groups such as 'Empowering uniqueness' as well as borderline stalking culture 'I am Looking for You'. Being the two groups that transverse both sexes, 'Beautiful People Connect' and 'Cheaper Living NZ' could express the socio-cultural climate of what would be an Auckland demographic. Interestingly, under 'Women' and 'Gender' there was a range of groups for the female ranging from 'Early ultrasound Prediction' to 'Gutsy Women Circle', but only one for the male. The top 10 related tags stayed identical besides the Identity and Relationships category where 'Single Parent' and 'Relationships' (Female) standing in for 'Love' and 'Socialising' (Male).

United States (US)

When using VPN to access the same accounts from America the results drastically changed. Upon entering the interface under female, the first "suggested" page presented was 'Donald J.

Figure removed due to copyright issues

Figure 3

Trump' (Fig 3.) – who had just won the 2017 presidential election where most people got their news from Facebook (PEW, 2017). As stated before, the 'create group' button is now appearing for the female account, Overall, the groups suggested are less '18+' sexualised than NZ but had strong tones of religion and monogamy with groups like 'Single Christian men and women for mature relationships', 'Meet Christian Singles Dating or Friendship Site' and 'Revert Muslims Want Marry'. In juxtaposition, there is also strong themes of foreign or 'Exotic Dating' spanning across both sexes and all categories. Like with NZ, groups are not listed in order of membership: 'Hot Zone +18' (33,949) followed by 'Secrets' (44,665). Only 2 groups, as opposed to NZ's 3 went across sexes and categories: 'Exotic Dating and 'Born Again'. Related tags also only differentiated under the 'Identity and Relationships' category, where 'Girlfreind' and 'Online Dating' (female) stand in for 'Women' and 'Engagement' (male). Interestingly, the Gender category could not be found when accessing from the US, which poses questions to weather it was *Facebook's* choice (like with suggested groups) or down to demographics.

TABLE 3
AGE: 25
LOCATION:
NZ/USA

14

	MALE (NZ)	MALE (US)
IDENTITY AND RELATIONSHIPS	1. Australian Flirting & Encounter's 2. Real Singles 30+ New Zealand Only 3. SINGLESCREW 4. Singles NZ - 18yo+ only Friendships; Single parent; Weddings; Love; Family; Marriage; Women; Relationships; LGTB; Wedding Photography	1. I'm Dz And I'm Free To Express MySelf 2. The cultural of a Deaf friendly world CDFW 3. Forever friends 4. vento da natureza Friendship; Love; Marriage; Dating; Online dating service; Family; Women; Escorpio; Love
RELATIONSHIPS	1. Secret Men's Business 2. Born Again 3. Esoteric Tantra 4. Flame Couples Ministry Love; Dating; Marriage; Friendship; Women; Online dating service; Polyamory; Spirituality; Singles group; Romance	1. Single Girls 2. erectile dysfunction discussion 3. Age Gap Dating 4. Social Classifieds Canada United States Toronto Montreal New York Houston (")
LOVE	1. Massey Presbyterian Church 2. CHILL 3. The Australian Way of the Superior Man 4. PYAR AN DOSTI Friendship; Dating; Relationships; Marriage; Relationship; Happiness; God; Music: Spirituality; Family	1. USA||CANADA||AUSTRALIA||UK Friends Club 2. Art of Living 3. I Promise Never Hurt You 4. Love Girls (")
FRIENDSHIP	1. B'oz R18 2. Real Singles 30+ New Zealand Only 3. Kiwi Singles Crew R30 4. Laugh,Let Go, Wahoo Love: Dating; Family: Chatear; Music; Funny; Support; Having fun; Happiness; Relationships	1. USA||CANADA||AUSTRALIA||UK Friends Club 2. Young generation 3. MY HEART WILL GO ON!!!!!!!!!!! 4. Make new friends international (")
WOMEN	1. Equal Opportunity Science - Australia Entrepreneurship; Empowerment; Networking; Business; Christian; Friendship; Leader; Feminism; Spirituality; Love	1. I love blond women 2. Looking for Love and Ending Your Single Life 3. Lonely women looking for life partner to live together without marriage 4. White women & Black Men – Serious Dating (")
GENDER	1. Trans IQ2ed Love; Friendship; Chatear; Relationships; Friendship; Marriage; Online Dating Service; Singles group; Singles; Single Women	N/A

Age: 25
Findings

As the table shows, the 25 Female was
unable to be used. Surprisingly, *Facebook*
blocked access and required the female,
as opposed to the male, to send in a
picture of herself (Fig. 4). This could be
for one of many reasons. Potentially,

Figure removed due to copyright issues

Figure 4

Facebook crosschecks with facial recognition software as a security measure, in an environment where up to an estimated %40 of accounts is fake. Facebook's statement reads that the photo will 'be permanently deleted from our server' but as (Dorsch et al 2016) points out, 'Facebook's database never "forgets" anything' (Andrejevic 2013). Whatever the reason, Facebook requires photo verification from 25-year-old females and not males, and we know that they are upgrading and updating their facial recognition technologies (MIT Technology Review, 2017). Besides this, the Interface behaved in the exact same way as 13 years.

New Zealand (NZ)

Unlike comparing sexes, when it comes to countries there are no groups that correlate. This could mean that Facebook's algorithm concerning suggested groups could depend more on the location of where the user rather than the person's sex, name, and age. Like with 13 years, the 25-year-old male groups appear to be influenced by neighbouring country Australia: 'Australian Flirting & Encounters', 'Australian Way of the Superior Man' and 'Equal Opportunity Science – Australia'. Again, there are strong themes of heteronormativity, targeting singles as every top suggested group under 'Identity and Relationships.' The algorithm has displaced groups focused on the age (25) supplied, however, most of the dating based groups are either '18+' or '30+'. Across both ages, sexes, and locations the related tags are are identical outside 'Identity and Relationships,' with 'Love' and 'Friendship' being the most related tag to the categories analysed. Like with 13 years, related tag differences show 'Single parent' and 'Wedding Photography' (NZ) in place for 'Love' and 'Love' (US).

United States (US)

Like with 13 years, the US groups displayed more tones of race and national identities: 'White women & Black Men – Serious Dating,' 'USA||CANADA||AUSTRALIA||UK Friends Club'. However, the 25-year-old male's groups were less suggestive towards religion monogamy: 'Lonely women looking for life partner to live together without marriage'.

Limits and Further Analyses

This analysis sees limits when trying to understand how and why a user would interact and react to such features and suggestions. Even after the controlled conditions undertaken, *Facebook* has vast technological mechanisms that could still detect my exact location i.e., The University of Auckland Library. These options for discovery also appear to be in constant flux, changing more as the service is being used more extensively (e.g. my own suggestions are targeted towards me). There is speculation about whether the algorithm is based on usage. We know the most popular groups are not listed numerically, but the related tags could be of the user's doing.

More studies over time will provide a quantitative analysis that will show how suggestions are changing, and, potentially, in ordnance to a given socio-cultural setting. Increasing the user numbers and countries involved will offer a more comprehensive result. Testing how joining groups could change the user-experience both on *Facebook* and the wider web (*Google Search*) could produce interesting results. New 'Custom Gender' is now offered as of 2014, allowing a pre-set of 71 options by *Facebook* (Agender, Androgyne, Androgynous, Bigender etc) as well as the option to add your own. Further analyses could focus on these custom gender options to see if they effect *Facebook's* algorithm.

Deconstructing the Alias

Through this analysis, we can see that Facebook is not operating in the interests of neutralising gender and sexual categorizations. To the country, and not according to popular user practices, Facebook is actively (re)categorizing based on the age, location, and sex of the user. Through such a motion, a *Facebook* user becomes computationally *aliased* as part of the SNS internetwork.

New media research language is required to transpose what is largely a world of mathematics and code. Studying the *alias* of a user's persona online, as outlined, focuses on the way information becomes part of this mathematical world – utilised in autonomous and internetworked machine-learning algorithms. Our changing relationship to sexuality, as with other socio-cultural forces under mediatisation, is seeing the dematerialization of the interface (Miller, 2015), in a world narrated by 'new' media savvy users but plotted, and ritualised, by profiteering big data companies and their computational logics. As part of the third wave of the internet (Case, 2016), big data is seeing identities being woven into the algorithmic fabric of SNSs. People are thinking, labeling and announcing their identity within a quantifying computational mesh, algorithmically soaking accumulative knowledge. These occult and well-guarded algorithms 'have thus come to serve as the new "gatekeepers" of public digital space' (Zittrain & Palfrey, 2006).

Our data footprint we accumulate throughout out lives is being embedded into the algorithmic nature of big data. This accumulation is 'doubling every two years,' seeing 'our lives gradually migrate onto the Internet' (Aiden & Michel, 2014:11). As we have explored with the use of SNS, as well as other network services, *aliasing* sees interpersonal frequencies or qualities processed under algorithmic logic and control (Kowalski, 1979). Big data captures "self-qualifying" users and discretely quantifies the signal in computational and media logics that can be the pedagogic consumption of algorithms.

The Algorithmic Life

To understand what this paper calls the "objective aptitudes" imposed by the digital incarnation of an algorithmic alias, Roberge et al (2016), focused on four types of digital information calculations that, metaphorically speaking, 'can be thought of as located *beside, above, within,* and *below* the mass of online digital data'. (p.8)

The volume or measurement of the popularity of, say unique or expected visitors in the form of "clicks", can be seen computationally operating *beside* the surface web. Located *above* the web is an internetworked 'authority of links recording and exchanging the 'recognition' signals among internet-users' (p.9). This top-down approach sees an internet service 'algorithm arranges information by considering that when a site is linked it is simultaneously receiving a token of recognition, which gives it more authority' (p.9). *Within* the web points to 'how users actively evaluate each other' under the confines of an often suggestive user-experience. The paradigmatic brand the 'like' (thumbs up), for example, is 'the most the size of personal networks by number of friends, reputation acquired from published articles and links others have subsequently shared or commented on, the number of times an Internet-user is mentioned in an online conversation, and so forth' (p.13).

As we have explored, the SNS is accommodating how Internet-users are making homogeneous choices, bringing together people whose tastes, interests, and opinions resemble their own' (p.15). Roberge et al conclude with *under* the web, where Internet services are 'recording the traces left by Inter-users as discreetly as possible'. (p.15)

EdgeRank

Facebook's spearheading algorithm *EdgeRank* works beside, above', within, and below the service, optimizing the user-experience. The SNS introduced the algorithm in 2010 shortly after it became open to the share market, whose purpose is to navigate, structure and prioritize a user's information as part of their individualised experience.

What we know is that this algorithm works in three-fold: user's *affinity* (how they relate to a given post by location, interaction etc.); the *weight* of content (amount of views, comments, likes etc.); *time-based* decay rates (how new or old the content is). However, Facebook has not released the supposed 21 other facets that formulate *EdgeRank's* algorithm. These facets encompass a can have broad implications for the user's experience: 'for instance, the selection can produce a filter bubble (if users are exposed to updates which confirm their opinions etc.) or alter people's mood (if users are shown a disproportionate amount of positive or negative updates' (Kjær Langvad, 2016:30). This click-bait approach mediatises and aliases social actions and practices in the service, focusing association and attention to content that has accumulated numerous reactions, sensational stories' where 'sensational stories are arguably bound to be over-represented' (p.32)

In such an algorithmic network dependent on aliasing, there are almost 40% of new *Facebook* profiles that are fake, created by malware writers and spammers (Chakraborty el al 2014). Arora & Schieber (2017) found that 'micro-fraud through false self-representations is committed on a quotidian basis across cultures as youth seek to optimize the digital sphere to maximize their desirability for their prospects' (p.418). These manufactured aliases, with often deceptive intent, are thus effecting the algorithmic filter bubble on the same computationally equal grounds as aliases that represent a genuine person.

Nexus of Practice

To deconstruct the aliasing effects an algorithm such as *Edgerank* has on user's information is a question of symbolic *engagement, navigation,* and *change.* Scollon & Scollon (2002) theorise a nexus of practice as 'the ways in which people engage each other in communication through a very wide range of material supports and extensions from the structure of the built environment and its furniture and to the media by which communication may be moved across distance of time and space' (p.4).

The practice *circumferencing* the alias computationally constructs an interdependent network from which the signal passes through, creating an algorithmic discourse or displacement. These "discourse cycles" are analysed to calculate 'the trajectories of participants, places, and situations both back in time historically and forward' (p.9). Under the quantity of data flowing through CMC, this discursive change is symbolically charged, affording SNS users to navigate a seemingly limitless site of engagement.

A nexus of practice amalgamates from a repetitive social action at such a site, changing, over time, how the action is symbolically understood i.e., causing "semiotic cycles" that influence variations in discursive and motivational evaluations of the user. This accumulative spiral effect changes the nexus of practice, conceptualising a *zone of identification* that pulls in other social actions and practices: a full Nexus. The study of SNS as a full Nexus will shed light on a user's algorithmic life, how semiotics and discourse behave in such a way as to invisibly transform social life. Within a computational framework, a nexus of practice theorizes the alias as a *historical body*: 'different people play the same role differently depending on their history of personal experience inscribed' (p.9)

Actor-network Theory

The Actor-network theory (ANT): 'analysis focuses not only on 'stuff' – the objects and materials that make the semiotic work interpretation possible' (Haugaard & Clegg 2009) as with theorized in the nexus of practice. ANT sees the 'presumption behind every action lies an *intention*' (p.2). Unlike social practice, ANT studies power - how *agencement* or association are effected system-like power structures. Like in Foucault's 'The subject and power' (1982), with his allegory of the mode's power involved in the panoptic control of the prison through its own prisoners, the actor-network is comprised on powers of association. ANT does not focus on the alias' 'intentions, will or consciousness' but its effects in panoptic power relations: 'the focus is on a *transfer from visible forms of power to the invisible*, particularly that which accomplishes a transfer of the duties of supervision from hierarchy to self '(p.5).

The "Social-network Theory" sees services like *Facebook* become the intermediaries of a panoptic 'non-human' idea of power, where aliasing 'pre-figures' (Strathern 1992) or 'emplaces' (Heidesgger 1993) the need for the systemic human agency. ANT points to the wider world beyond *Facebook*, however, 'across a whole variety of intuitions, including science, government, the factory and markets' (p.9). Big data now binds these institutions of power. The alias is the computationally *punctualised* (Munro 2004) version of the user, an identity that, 'not only takes an intensely local character; it also becomes timed' (p.11). This time-stamped alias causes 'action at a distance' that is the invisible 'Other', algorithmically controlling the power associations whereby an actor is networked. Deconstructing the alias with the theories as outlined will help move scientific world of powers into the language of human sciences. One purpose for mediatisation research is to translate such methodologies as outlined into a tangible and theoretical language. To envelope the sexual in 'Sexual Alias', we must not only test services like *Facebook* treat sexual from *within* but how "communicative sexualities" are interacting and communicating *with* the SNS.

Social Network Sexualities

The findings are in ordnance with recent scholarly work that has investigated sexual conventions and practices moving into an online communicative environment. Through the SNS, sexuality and sexual identity are now an embedded media practice. Hilton-Morrow & Battles, (2015) introduces sexuality as a categorization process. Sexual identity and language are constructed and managed, 'continually in flux as cultural meanings are continually negotiated' (p. 10). This negotiating of norms in the construction and management of sexual identity on SNS presents an insightful perspective into media-embedded forces that normalise certain behaviors, orientations, and desires.

Martiniz (2011) talks of the sexual life-world now being one of plurality, communication, and cosmopolitanism. The sexual experience is constantly being meaningfully negotiated under an array of embodied realities. This *communicology* of sexualities sees 'the phenomenon of sexuality within the intricacies of our immediate and embodied interconnection with the social and cultural world in which we are situated' (p.11). As we have explored, the socio-cultural world is moving online and *situating* people's online sexuality in dematerialised social realities. Martinez proceeds to the connect the semiotic phenomenology of *communicative sexualities* to the generation of socio-sexual codes, stating that when 'we talk about sexuality, we are most certainly talking about desire' (p.101). These heterosexual-homosexual binaries on SNS are the result of communicative sexualities (self)determining desire.

Performing (Sexual) Desirability

In her work 'Bodies That Matter' (2003), Judith Butler proclaims 'the misapprehension about gender performativity is this: that gender is a choice, or that gender is a role, or that gender is a construction that one puts on, as one puts on clothes in the morning, that there is a 'one' who is prior to this gender, a one who goes to the wardrobe of gender and decides with deliberation which gender it will be today.' The wardrobe of gender and gender deliberation is now virtually in the hands of SNSs, (dis)playing an array of sexually charged affordances to accommodate the 'one'. The SNS thus categories and equips the tools needed to perform (sexual) desirability. Examining sexual discourse sees 'the foundational categories of identity – the binary of sex, gender, and the body – can be shown as productions that create the effect of the natural, the original and the inevitable' (Butler 1990a: viii).

The body, therefore, is the site of sexual materialization, moulded by a symbolic hierarchy of norms and values that the SNS has appropriated into a performing (dis)play of desirability. 'The cyberself' (Robinson, 2007) and the (de)construction of sexual identity(s) thus appears to be an act of performance. Through the paper's analyses, we can see *Facebook* is inscribing a performing act of desirability that is sexually skewed – in the form of categorically sexualised suggestions and relations. This (dis)play is realised, or embodied, with a participatory online communicology rooted in the gender performativity and sexual self-identification.

This creative expression of one's image or persona is therefore confined to *act* of desirable (sexual) performativity. The communicology of desire, at least for Facebook, appears to be computationally sexualised – offering tools and suggesting tones of a binary heterosexual nature.

Servicing (Sexual) Desire

The SNSs are thus used as an instrument for desirability and the interpolation of desire. This kind of instrumental desire is 'meant to include wishes about how the past might have been as well as desires for the present and future, and to include sensuous along with intellectual goals' (Schroeder 2001). With the nature of the SNS as outlined, a person's intrinsic desire is being symbiotically acted out or performed with the accommodations and affordances permitted. Biologically, our desires are connected to 'both positive reward signals (increased dopamine in response to an intuitive reward) and negative punishment signals (decreased dopamine in response to the failure of an expected reward to appear)' (Shultz 1998). The given SNS must control these signals to keep the user servicing their desires, not only achieved on an algorithmic level as this paper has analysed, but an array of customizable servicing tools.

The profile image, as Ortiz (2016) found, is used to 'present their public image as a set of works of art, or opera' (p.41). The profile image can be surveyed by anyone despite privacy settings and, through a single photo, encapsulates the user's life-story. The agency over such a choice of photo is 'attached to a set of rules, protocols, and conditions of interaction and communication offered by this new technological environment' (p.59). Barthel (2017) saw how 'sexualized photos and female photos were perceived as more attractive' (p.63) and the comments and messages on such photos 'focus[ed] on promiscuous behavior, sexualized body imagery and fashion standards, and body uncertainty or preoccupation' (p.73)

Rubin & McClelland's (2015) 'Even though it's a small checkbox, it's a big deal', where they study how 'situational and interpersonal factors in shaping management of sexuality in digital contexts' (p.513) are inducing certain conventions and psychological implications of managing identity (s). This can be realised with studies showing women post more pictures than men (Vanderhoven 2014) and are more likely to post on themes of cuteness or romance (Peluchette & Karl 2008).

Mediatisation of Desire

Proponents of mediatisation call attention to the paradigmatic shift in power relations and negotiating factors when encoding/decoding a media text (Hall, 1980). As we have explored, the computational and media logic– 'the institutional and technological modus operandi of the media' (Hjarvard, 2008, p. 113)' - has taken an introverted leap into a person's desirably lived-experience. Indeed, your social media life can even start before birth, with the sharing of fetal ultrasound images now a common practice' (Lupton 2013).

The SNS inhibits social change (Shultz 1999;2003), offering extension (across barriers like distance and time), substitution (mitigates offline interaction), amalgamation (draws into non-mediated interaction) and accommodation (adaption to media practices). With the rise and consolidation of a handful of SNSs, the conceptual boundaries of a free agency when using platforms such as Facebook are coming to a definitive end; what was the democratisation is now the mediatisation of desire.

As we have explored, a combination of mediatisation and computational logics have sexualised desirability in SNS. McNair (2002) saw how operations of media became an attempt 'to integrate the aesthetics of pornography into the non-pornographic forms of art….and promotional culture (p.81). Although the GUI and aesthetics of, say *Facebook*, appear modern, sleek and professional, its computational mechanisms are integrating the aesthetics of a such a promoted culture. The theme under the veneer of mundane internetworked social meditation, are signals whose 'frequency involves ordinary people talking about sex and their own sexualities, revealing intimate details of their feelings and their bodies in the public sphere' (p.88). Feelings, motivations, and desires are a thus conclusively under a process of mediatisation, pushing the conceptual boundaries of democratic will or free agency. Its mediatisation, not the media, that are proliferating 'a sexual economy and politics in which not only women and gays, but straight men are occupying different social positons than those to which they have been used' (p.206).

Society is presented with a myriad of challenges and issues when desire is primarily driven through a process of mediatisation. The ubiquity of 'New' media requires a new philosophical and interdisciplinary approach, as has been called for in contemporary media studies research (Hansen 2006). As people become more dependent on CMC to express themselves, social transformation will increasingly be subtle, more nuanced and, consequently, ambivalent. Indeed, most everyone who would read this paper (including myself) has a compromised perspective as they are directly (or indirectly) a *part* of computational logics and control. New media, largely accelerated by the SNS, socio-culturally encumbers people's collective understand and comprehend of themselves. Through the endowed aptitudes of a computer-mediated life, people are beginning to negate and qualify themselves. This *negation of negation* sees a contradictory climate where social change is a voluntary and participatory position and imposition taken with and within CMC.

Below we will briefly theorise on different disciplinary thought regarding the implications of mediatised world, where human qualities – identity, sexuality, desires and conceptions thereof – are hereafter media-embedded processes.

Crises of Individuation

Having a person's wants, goals or purpose set through mediatisation has major psychological implications. For Jungian psychology, individuation is procedural i.e., 'the capacity for adaptation: the individual either focuses excessively on his interior environment or neglects it entirely in his efforts to adapt to the external environment' (Chabot p.110). Individuation, in other words, is the harmony between "external" selfless-qualification and "internal self-qualification – reaching a balanced "new state" (Jung 1932) that unites two incomplete halves of the psyche. With the mediatisation of desire and categorisation of the Self online, the balance between these psychological stimuli are centralising around the externality of SNS. Jung maintained that some innate biological forces, or 'subjective aptitudes' afflicted the individuation process, however, with mediatisation these forces are spilling over into artificial life.

Social life is now contending with media-embedded "objective aptitudes". The convergence of these two forces are forging a new individual "mode of existence" (Simondon 1989). Taking Jung's theory further, Simondon theorises that individuation sees 'this individual sacrifices to the social game, meeting the 'inter-individual…a society that is well organised, but lacking in authenticity' (Chabot p.99). This lack of true authentication makes the desire to self-authenticate through SNS compromised and unfulfilling: "people who had taken a break from Facebook felt happier and were less sad and lonely". (Happiness Research Institute, 2015)

Surveillance and Stalking Culture

Through the mediatisation of desire, the voluntary nature of normalised mass-surveillance being mundanely performed is becoming the norm. Andrejevic (2007) explores this growing culture to spy on one another – 'a nation of watchers performing their verification practices with an eye to the gaze of an imagined other, in order to avoid being seen as a dupe' (p.240). We live in a quantifying society, intermittently drawing into a voyeuristic (dis)play of desirability. Stalking cultures have the implication of becoming common social practice i.e, finding out one another's identities, sexuality and desires through eavesdropping on someone's online presence and persona will make first impressions are predetermined and predisposed by mediatisation. This 'imagined other' is a conjured (dis)illusion, inverting verifiable and authentic social traditions as a form of a virtual social-media-reality. The use of stalking on SNS is a kind of 'lateral surveillance' (Andrejevic 2007:223), whose implications forebode a voyeuristic global village that loses face to online stalking and interaction.

Symbolical Mastery

In a social world fuelled by the mediatisation of desire, symbolic efficiency will be controlled and managed by the cybernetic SNS; meaning will take an "algorithmic turn" (Uricchio, 2011). As Zizek aptly laments, 'this suspension of the function of the (symbolic) Master is the crucial feature of the Real whose contours loom at the horizon of the cyberspace universe: the moment of implosion when humanity will attend the limit impossible to transgress' (p.802). People have the potential, in other words, to fall into a "not quite spectral enough" social universe that has the power to change meaningful conceptions of what 'Real' is by mostly artificial means. For Zizek, the characteristics of cyberspace, which can largely by equated to SNSs, 'hinges on the network of socio-symbolic relations (of power and domination, etc.) which always-already overdetermine the way cyberspace affects us.' (p.829). This presents an *ontological paradox for the absolute desire.*

Displaced (Self)Mediators

Amongst her work on *communicative capitalism*, Dean (2002) emphasizes how production and consumption drives 'an ideological formation that uses democracy, creativity, access, and interconnection to produce the subjects of communicative capitalism' (p.103). Forces of a liberal post-capitalist power structure have consolidated (inter)information, and desire, as a form of consumption, or servicing. In her book named Blog Theory, Dean talks 'of the term "displaced mediators" designates mediators whose functions have been displaced from what appears (retroactively) as the previous role'. The mediatisation of desire could implicate the user, (re)producer, or agent of social media as a displaced mediator. The user's initial function was to socialise with an SNS but under the forces, as outlined, has been displaced by a computational alias whose role is to feed economic and algorithmic growth. Social media users are self-mediating their own displacement in a service that ends up using the user.

Conclusion

The social media service (SNS) is a symbiotic relationship between user wants and service needs, 'providing stability and meaning to social behavior' (Scott, 2012:15) whilst relying on the expropriation of such behaviors to service user wants, motivations and desires – to encourage meaningful user-generation and mediation.

Therefore, the use of CMC, as outlined through SNSs, is feeding a new breed of technological consumption i.e., 'what consumers wanted, from their deepest desires and fantasies to their more transient preferences and fancies, would be gathered, compiled, analysed, and delivered' (Dead, 2002:63). SNSs are therefore dependent on tactics that will increase usage and the free flow of interpersonal information.

The user analyses found that *Facebook* is attempting to modulate a user's 'lived traditions' of sexuality into 'symbolic content' (Hepp, 2012). The SNS is 'reorganizing places as media spaces' (Couldry, 2004), foreboding a sexually lived experience being controlled by the mediatisation of desire – a social network rooted in a kind of technological sexual determinism. This paper, along with recent leaks of *Facebook's* rule book (Helft, 2017), proves that SNS is acting out adverse biases. The company has even been found doing ethnographic studies of their own user base to commercially target vulnerabilities and anxieties (Smith, 2017)

The paper attempted to formulate a better perspective of the wider 'world beyond Facebook' (Lovink, 2016:37). Mediatization is interested in this wider world i.e., how CMC has fostered prevailing intimate cultures – 'how people give meaning to gender, sexuality, relationships, and desire' (de Ridder & Bauwell, 2015:1) – through social media. The psychological and computational developments attached to such changes are symbiotically (re)embodying a heteronormative sexual archetype that must be investigated further.

Acknowledgements

I would like to thank the guidance and recommendations of my professor as well as and my colleagues for meaningful and enlightening discussions.

References

Andrejevic, M. (2007). iSpy: Surveillance and power in the interactive era (pp. vii-325). Lawrence: University Press of Kansas.

Andrejevic, M. (2013). Public service media utilities: Rethinking search engines and social networking as public goods. Media International Australia, 146(1), 123-132.

Antin, J., Yee, R., Cheshire, C., & Nov, O. (2011, October). Gender differences in Wikipedia editing. In Proceedings of the 7th international symposium on Wikis and open collaboration (pp. 11-14). ACM.

Arora, P., & Scheiber, L. (2017). Slumdog romance: Facebook love and digital privacy at the margins. Media, Culture & Society, 39(3), 408-422.

Boryczka, J. M. (2017). An Anatomy of Sexism: The Colonized Vagina. New Political Science, 39(1), 36-57.

Butler, J. (2011). Bodies that matter: On the discursive limits of sex. Taylor & Francis.

Case, Steve. The Third Wave: An Entrepreneur's Vision of the Future. N.p., (2016). Print.Chicago Cohen, J. E. (2012). Configuring the networked self: Law, code, and the play of everyday practice. Yale University Press.

Chabot, P. (2013). The philosophy of Simondon: Between technology and individuation. A&C Black.

Chakraborty, M., Pal, S., Pramanik, R., & Chowdary, C. R. (2016). Recent developments in social spam detection and combating techniques: A survey. Information Processing & Management, 52(6), 1053-1073.

Cheney-Lippold, J. (2011). A new algorithmic identity: Soft biopolitics and the modulation of control. Theory, Culture & Society, 28(6), 164-181.

Chicago

Clegg, S. R., & Haugaard, M. (Eds.). (2009). The Sage handbook of power. Sage.

Cohen, J. E. (2012). Configuring the networked self: Law, code, and the play of everyday practice. Yale University Press.

Conference on (pp. 1-4). IEEE.

Constine, J. (2012, August 22). How Big Is Facebook's Data? 2.5 Billion Pieces Of Content And 500 Terabytes Ingested Every Day. Retrieved June 12, 2017, from https://techcrunch.com/2012/08/22/how-big-is- facebooks- data-2-5-billion-pieces-of-content-and- 500-terabytes-ingested-every-day/

Couldry, N., & Hepp, A. (2013). Conceptualizing mediatization: Contexts, traditions, arguments. Communication Theory, 23(3), 191-202.

Couldry, N., & McCarthy, A. (2004). Mediaspace: Place, scale and culture in a media age. Rutledge. Dean, J. (2002). Publicity's secret: How technoculture capitalizes on democracy. Cornell University Press. Dean, J. (2010). Blog theory: Feedback and capture in the circuits of drive. Polity. Dean, J. (2013). Society doesn't exist. First Monday, 18(3).

De Ridder, S. (2017). Mediatization and sexuality: An invitation to a deep conversation on values, communicative sexualities, politics and media.

De Ridder, S., & Van Bauwel, S. (2015). The discursive construction of gay teenagers in times of mediatization: youth's reflections on intimate storytelling, queer shame and realness in popular social media places. Journal of Youth Studies, 18(6), 777-793.

De Ridder, S., & Van Bauwel, S. (2015). Youth and intimate media cultures: Gender, sexuality, relationships, and desire as storytelling practices in social networking sites. Communications, 40(3), 319-340.

Deuze, M. (2014). Media Life and the Mediatization of the Lifeworld. In Mediatized Worlds (pp. 207- 220). Palgrave Macmillan UK.

Domingos, P. (2015). The master algorithm: How the quest for the ultimate learning machine will remake our world. Basic Books.

Dorsch, I., & Ilhan, A. (2016). Photo Publication Behavior of Adolescents on Facebook. Facets of Facebook: Use

Duguay, S. (2016). "He has a way gayer Facebook than I do": Investigating sexual identity disclosure and context collapse on a social networking site. new media & society, 18(6), 891-907.

Duguay, S. (2017). Dressing up Tinderella: interrogating authenticity claims on the mobile dating app Tinder. Information, Communication & Society, 20(3), 351-367.

Dunlop. (2017, May 30). Who Owns Facebook? - The 10 Richest Facebook Shareholders. Retrieved June 12, 2017, from https://www.incomediary.com/who-owns-facebook- the-10-richest-facebook-shareholders

Ekström, M., Fornäs, J., Jansson, A., & Jerslev, A. (2016). Three tasks for mediatization research: contributions to an open agenda. Media, Culture & Society, 0163443716664857.

Facebook DataCenter, Servers and Infrastructure FAQ. (n.d.). Retrieved June 12, 2017, from http://www.datacenterknowledge.com/the- facebook-data-center-faq/

Foucault, M. (1982). The subject and power. Critical inquiry, 8(4), 777-795.

Google Search Statistics. (n.d.). Retrieved June 12, 2017, from http://www.internetlivestats.com/google- search-statistics/#sources

Hall, S. (1980). Encoding/decoding, s 128-138 i Hall, S, Hobson, D, Lowe, A & Willis, P (red) Culture. Media. Language.

Hansen. New Philosophy for New Media. The MIT Press, 2006.

Heller, L., & Goodman, L. (2016, October). What do avatars want now? Posthuman embodiment and the technological sublime. In Virtual System & Multimedia (VSMM), 2016 22nd International Conference on (pp. 1- 4). IEEE.

Hepp, A. (2012). Mediatization and the 'molding force' of the media. Communications, 37(1), 1-28. Hepp, A., & Krotz, F.. (2014). Mediatized worlds: Culture and society in a media age. Springer. Hill, D. W. (2013). Avatar ethics: Beyond images and signs. Journal for Cultural Research, 17(1), 69- Hilton-Morrow, W., Battles, K. (2015). Sexual Identities and the Media: An Introduction. Rutledge.

Helft, Matt. (2017) "Facebook Users Who Are Under Age Raise Concerns". Nytimes.com. N.p., 2017. Web. 19 June 2017.

Hughes, J., Morrison, L., & Thompson, S. (2016). Who Do You Think You Are? Examining the Off/Online Identities of Adolescents Using a Social Networking Site. In Youth 2.0: Social Media and Adolescence (pp. 3-19). Springer International Publishing.

Illadis, A., & Russo, F. (2016). Critical data studies: An introduction. Big Data & Society, 3(2), 2053951716674238.

Jansson, A. (2015). The molding of mediatization: The stratified indispensability of media in close relationships. Communications, 40(4), 379-401.

Kjær Langvad, R. (2016). Connected by Loneliness.

MIT Technology Review. (2017, April 06). In China, you can pay for goods just by showing your face. Retrieved June 19, 2017, from https://www.technologyreview.com/s/603494/10-breakthrough-technologies-2017-paying-with-your-face/

Kowalski, R. (1979). Algorithm= logic+ control. Communications of the ACM, 22(7), 424-436.

Krotz, F. (2009). Mediatization: A concept with which to grasp media and societal change. Mediatization: Concept, changes, consequences, 21-40.

Larsen, M. C. (2016). An 'Open Source'Networked Identity. On Young People's Construction and Co- construction of Identity on Social Network Sites. In Youth 2.0:

Social Media and Adolescence (pp. 21- 39). Springer International Publishing.

Lovink, G. (2016). Social Media Abyss: Critical Internet Cultures and the Force of Negation. John Wiley & Sons.

Lupton, D. (2013). The social worlds of the unborn. Springer.

Mager, A. (2012). Algorithmic ideology: How capitalist society shapes search engines. Information, Communication & Society, 15(5), 769-787.

Markman, J. (2016, June 13). Facebook, Microsoft And The Cloud Under The Sea. Retrieved June 12, 2017, from https://www.forbes.com/sites/jonmarkman/2016/06/13/facebook-microsoft-and-the-cloud-under-the- sea/#4c1f9edd4480

Martinez, J. M. (2011). Communicative sexualities: A communicology of sexual experience. Lexington Books.

Mazzoleni, G., & Schulz, W. (1999). " Mediatization" of politics: A challenge for democracy?. Political communication, 16(3), 247-261.

McGlotten, S. (2013). Virtual intimacies: Media, affect, and queer sociality. Suny Press. McNair, B. (2002). Striptease culture: Sex, media and the democratization of desire. Psychology Press. McNair, B. (2013). Porno? Chic!: How pornography changed the world and made it a better place. Rutledge. Olshausen, B. A. (2000). Aliasing. PSC 129–Sensory Processes, 3-4.

Rheingold, H. (1993). The virtual community: Finding commection in a computerized world. Addison- Wesley Longman Publishing Co., Inc.

Rueda-Ortiz, R., & Giraldo, D. (2016). Profile Image: Ways of Self-(re-) presentation on the Facebook Social Network. In Youth 2.0: Social Media and Adolescence (pp. 41-60). Springer International Publishing.

Roberge, J., & Seyfert, R. (2016). What are algorithmic cultures? (pp. 1-25). R. Seyfert, & J. Roberge (Eds.). Abingdon: Rutledge.

Robinson, L. (2007). The cyberself: the self-ing project goes online, symbolic interaction in the digital age. New Media & Society, 9(1), 93-110.

Schroeder, T. (2004). Three faces of desire. Oxford University Press.

Schulz, W. (2004). Reconstructing mediatization as an analytical concept. European journal of communication, 19(1), 87-101.

Scollon, S. W. (2004). Nexus analysis: Discourse and the emerging internet. Routledge.actor-network theory

Scott, J. (2012). Social network analysis. Sage.

Seyfert, R., & Roberge, J. (Eds.). (2016). Algorithmic Cultures: Essays on Meaning, Performance and New Technologies. Rutledge.

Simondon, G. (1989). Du mode d'existence des objets techniques.

Smith, M. (2017, May 01). Facebook able to target emotionally vulnerable teens for ads. Retrieved June 19, 2017, from http://www.networkworld.com/article/3193382/security/leaked-document-shows-how-facebook-can- target-emotionally-vulnerable-teens-for-ads.html

Steijn, W. M. P. (2016). The role of informational norms on social network sites. In Youth 2.0: Social Media and Adolescence (pp. 117-137). Springer International Publishing.

Uricchio, W. (2011). The algorithmic turn: Photosynth, augmented reality and the changing implications of the image. Visual Studies, 26(1), 25-35.

Wakeford, N. (2003). Research Note: Working with New Media's Cultural Intermediaries. Information, Communication & Society, 6(2), 229-245.

Walrave, M., Ponnet, K., Vanderhoven, E., Haers, J., & Segaert, B. (2016). Youth 2.0: Social Media and Adolescence.

Weeks, J. (2011). The languages of sexuality. Rutledge.

Zittrain, J., & Palfrey, J. (2008). Reluctant Gatekeepers: Corporate Ethics on a Filtered Internet. Access Denied: The Practice and Policy of Global Internet.

Zizek, S. (2004). What can psychoanalysis tell us about cyberspace?. The Psychoanalytic Review, 91(6), 801- 830.